zendoodle coloring

Fantastic Creatures

D1385318

Other great books in the series

zendoodle coloring

zendoodle coloring

Fantastic Creatures

Majestic Beings to Color and Display

illustrations by

Antonia Cardella

ST. MARTIN'S GRIFFIN

NEW YORK

ZENDOODLE COLORING: FANTASTIC CREATURES

Copyright © 2017 by St. Martin's Press. All rights reserved. Printed in the United States of America.
For information, address St. Martin's Press, 175 Fifth Avenue, New York, N.Y. 10010.

www.stmartins.com

ISBN 978-1-250-14911-4 (trade paperback)

Our books may be purchased in bulk for promotional, educational, or business use.
Please contact your local bookseller or the Macmillan Corporate and Premium
Sales Department at 1-800-221-7945, extension 5442, or by e-mail
at MacmillanSpecialMarkets@macmillan.com.

First Edition: January 2018

10 9 8 7 6